Life

Louise Romana Wade

BookLeaf
Publishing

Presentation by *BookLeaf Publishing*

Web: www.bookleafpub.com

E-mail: info@bookleafpub.com

ISBN: 9789357697347

First edition 2022

DEDICATION

The poems I have written are dedicated to my cat, Hector. He really allows me to feel alive and is always there for me. Thank you Hector.

Beginnings

I don't know what I'm doing.
I just gave it a try
But I'm giving it my best.
Oh the time has flown by.

I'm not good at poetry.
It's definitely an art.
But I'm giving it a go,
And doing my part.

Now where should I start?
How do I begin?
Writing's not easy.
I'll start from within.

These rhymes just come out
I like how it's going.
It feels like it's easier
Once the words all start flowing.

Now another bunch more
To fill up this book.
Just please enjoy them
And have a good look.

Hector

Hector is my cat, but he's also my boy.
Everything he does brings me so much joy.
Can a cat really save a person's life?
The world before him seemed so full of strife.
Only he could bring me the love that I needed.
Restoring me to normality, he really succeeded.

How can I write this without sounding cheesy?
Entertaining an audience is not really easy.
Can't understate the love I have for him.
The cuddles he gives always make me grin.
Oh the times we've had riding the train.
Really glad he doesn't make me chase him in from
the rain.

Hector's my life and means so much to me.
Each day spent with him I just feel so free.
Cats can be funny and amazing pets.
They make me spend money each month at the vets.
Oh I wish he'll be with me forever and ever.
Really need him so much because he is so clever.

8.54

Pie.
I
like
a
crust
flavoured
by
fruits.
Taste
the
fruit
fillings
evaporate
lightly.
Beautiful
joy
in
the
pleasant
meat
lining.
It
tastes
like
pie.

Inches

The voices.
They scream.
 Need quiet.
They hurt.
They 're loud.
They won't go away.
I can stop them with a drink.
It's hard to swallow.
It tastes bad.
The voices quieten.
I'm slowly getting peace.
Keep drinking.
Make them leave.
It's working.
Mug is empty.
Pain is leaving.
I feel free.
The panic sets in.
I need help.
Please help me.
I'm not ready to go.

Constant

Who am I?
What am I doing?
Am I happy?
Can I be the best me?
Where is my future going?
What do I want?
Why do I care what others think?
When will adulthood arrive?
What do you get when you multiply six by nine?
Am I wasting my time?
Where do I see myself in five years?
What is the point of being alive?
Have I lived a good life?
Will I be remembered if I'm gone?
How long do I have left?
Is there anything worth living for?
Who do I want to be?
What do I want for dinner?

Cat

Soft
Cuddly
Balls of fluff

Scratchy
Itchy
Claws so tough

Fast
Slender
Legs so long

Smelly
Fishy
Breath so strong

Grippy
Rough
Tongues that lap

Snoring
Gentle
Balls that nap

Wobbly
Hungry
Bellies of fat

But most
Importantly
I love my cat

Numbers

Add, subtract,
Multiply, divide
Facing a challenge
To which some may

Numbers that always
Seem to fascinate me.
Pi, root two, phi,
Zero, I, e.

Ensuring I remember
How to write proofs.
Numbers don't lie,
They just reveal truths.

Mathematicians thanks
For all that you've done.
When it comes to scientists,
You're all number one.

Stations

Long names of town can be hard to remember
Like when it's cooled in November and December
A publicity stunt from 1869
Now it's most known for the very long sign
For a laugh you could go there by train
A fun day out, even in the rain
If you get to go then try not to forget
Remember to wear a comfy jacket
Please just have fun if you go see this town
Won't be so much fun if you're feeling quite down
Located up on the Isle of Anglesey
Long way to go for me from Caerphilly
Going there is something I want to do
When I'm not ill and suffering from flu
You'll have to get a photo on the platform
Nicely wrapped up because it's not that warm
Go and enjoy yourself if you visit
You'll have a great time it'll be a great hit
Let's end this poem early but without a last rhyme
Llanfairpwllgwyngyllgogerychwyrndrobwllllantysili
ogogogoch

Rooted

A
Root.
A
Part
Of
A
Wet
Tuber.
Growth
Of
The
Lengthy
End.

Travelling

Physicians travelling in time
Adventures await
Not possible to complete
Intricate storytelling
CDs piling up

My time well spent
On fantastical voyages
Over history and the future
Never ending

eNumbers

Oh
Numbers.
A
Constant
If
Enormous.
A
Crossing
Of
Dynamics
Over
These
Quadrants.

This
Maths
Of
The
Jazzy
Fun
Manner.

If
Acurate,
Numbers

Find
Answers.
I
Saw
The
Maths
In
Entire
Novels
Of
Time.
Equations,
Numbers,
Puzzles
Their
Answers
My
Goal.

Cephalopods

Shooting cephalopods
Questioning nothing
Under pressure
It's just a game
Daily grinding
Over and over
Completing catalogues
Totally rewarding
Octoling superiority
Players to beat
Until the sequel
Splatoon 3

Photography

15

Gone are the shots that are easy to take.
A challenge even to capture a cake.
My joy from the photos is hard to fake.
Even though there's not anything at stake.

But I like the challenge, yes I do.
Only thirty photos them it's all gone through.
Yet printing them is very exciting too.

Cameras have improved so much over time.
A charm that is had that's exclusively mine.
My short aren't that great but I share them online.
Everyone thinks that they just look sublime.
Really it's just something fun and that's fine.
Although I don't know how I'll make this all rhyme.

Pain

The pain is ongoing
I wish it would end
The doctors won't help
I need a good friend

The meds just do nothing
It just won't die down
I wish I could smile
But I'm stuck with a frown

Just make the pain stop
Make it please go away
I want to live without
This pain for one day

I need it to go
I just need a break
Because it's causing me
To make lots of mistakes

I'm constantly hurting
It feels like a curse
Then sometimes for no reason
It suddenly gets worse

Dinner

I like to eat
A lot of good food
And cooking gets me
In a very good mood

A varied diet
is fun to enjoy
But too much of the same
Feels like quite the killjoy

I get bored of some food
If it's served on repeat
So I sometimes am fussy
With what I like to eat

I'll eat a lot of thing
But I don't eat fish
So if cooking for me
You know what not to dish

But other than that
I do like a lot
So if you are cooking
Make sure it's hot

Cuddles

When I'm tired he's there for me.
When I'm sad he cheers me.
When I need someone to talk to he's there.
When I cry he heals me.
When I'm happy he wants to play.
When I need a hug he cuddles up to me.
When I'm on the train he travels with me.
When I'm out for a walk he's on my shoulders.
When I'm cold he warms me.
When I get home he watches for me.
When I eat he eats with me.
Hector's really the best cat for me.

Time

Time confuses me.
It runs out so fast.
My life flashing before my eyes.
Existence gone in a blink.

The hours they pass by.
I feel like I'm speeding up.
Memories fade as new ones form.
Everything comes to an end.

Too fast then too slow.
Infinite yet short.
Millions of years been and gone.
Eons of the universe still to come.

The endless expansion.
I'll not understand it.
Momentarily it scares me.
Entirely forever.

Endings

I missed a few days
But this book's at an end.
I got ill early on
but I had time to mend.

Some poems came easy
whilst others did not
But I tried my best
To have some kind of plot

I hope that you liked
What I have said
But know I am tired
And going to bed

If you read all these
You may be confused
Reading some of these back
Even I'm quite bemused

But I tried my best
With a few different styles
But this is the last on
Possibly for a while

So thank you so much
For reading these rhymes
I did it for a challenge
Because that's fun sometimes.

Goodbye for now
I'll miss thinking of these
But my mind needs to relax
It's not easy to please.